This Gratitude Journal

Belongs to

_____

JOURNEY WELL

YOU ARE <u>MORE</u> THAN ENOUGH

GRATITUDE JOURNAL

MARIAH EDGINGTON BSN, RN
BYRON EDGINGTON ATP, CRMI

The SkyWriter Press
IOWA CITY

ISBN: 979-8-9854920-3-3

Book design: Jeremy Taylor (instagram.com/jeremy.taylor.ny)

Published by The SkyWriter Press in the United States of America

The SkyWriter Press
281 Danielle Street
Iowa City, Iowa 52245

www.mariahedgington.com
www.journeywellYAMTE.com
www.JWYAMTE.com
www.byronedgington.com

*Disclaimer: We offer no professional, psychological, mental health, or medical advice. We recognize that people have experienced terrible events in their history, tragedies that haunt them for the rest of their lives. We would never make light of those things or claim that *Journey Well* ignores those deeply damaging events. Please seek professional help. We include a list of resources and further study.

GRATITUDE JOURNAL

Gratitude Journaling will change your life.

Gratitude for what is already present in your life brings more abundance into your life. Gratitude is a mindset. Awareness plays an important part in this process. As you begin to notice things that work for you, you're able to weed out things that *do not*. By placing your focus on what you *do want*, the things that no longer serve you will fall away.

Creating new habits that become your new success paradigms is a focus-centered task, and not for the faint-hearted. These practices must be embraced fully to be woven into the fabric of your life. Daily practices must become your routine.

Self-love, kindness, compassion, GRATITUDE, and respect — are all for yourself initially. As these practices take hold in your life, they will settle deeper into your sub-conscious mind forming positive habits that will change your life forever. Today, make a list of the values and qualities you want in your life. From today forward choose them as your focus.

We journal in the morning and evening. We always give thanks for 5 -10 items that are present in our lives at this moment. It can be as simple as clean water, electricity, nourishing food, morning coffee, or a good book. We then proceed to a practice what we call *visioneering,* mentally seeing what we want in our lives — what we see for our future. This is followed by gratitude journaling stating our future desires. To begin, you'll state, "I'm so happy & grateful *now that* _____" You fill in what you envision, or visioneer, as your future. What do you want your future to be? By becoming aware of what you do want, having this daily practice, as well as a conviction that your desire can happen to/for you, you'll begin attracting this into your life.

Repeat this exercise several times to bring it into focus. This Gratitude Journal has been specially created to get you started. Launch your journey with this exciting ritual. Once it becomes a habit, feel free to purchase and use plain notebooks. We've filled more than we can count. One of the statements we wrote for several months has come true: "I'm so happy & grateful now that *Journey Well, You Are More Than Enough: (RE)Discover your passion, purpose, and love of yourself & life* is a Best Seller." Since you're reading it, you can see it works.

We fully expect results such as these for you, too. What you focus on expands. Make sure your speech, thoughts, and actions reflect what you want in your life. Dreams really can come true.

Fellow Traveler, we're grateful for you and wish you to
JOURNEY WELL,
Mariah & Byron

JOURNEY WELL, YOU ARE <u>MORE</u> THAN ENOUGH
GRATITUDE JOURNAL

I'm so happy and grateful for:

_____

_____

_____

I'm so happy & grateful *now* that:

_____

_____

_____

_____

_____

_____

_____

_____

_____

_____

_____

_____

_____

_____

_____

_____

_____

The universe speaks in the language of L.O.V.E. Level Of Vibrational Energy.

Gratitude will help keep that love high and sustain an amazingly rich life, in every way.

JOURNEY WELL, YOU ARE <u>MORE</u> THAN ENOUGH
GRATITUDE JOURNAL

I AM insightful

I'm so happy and grateful for:

_____
_____
_____

I'm so happy & grateful *now* that:

_____
_____
_____
_____
_____
_____
_____
_____
_____
_____
_____
_____
_____
_____
_____
_____
_____
_____

JOURNEY WELL, YOU ARE <u>MORE</u> THAN ENOUGH
GRATITUDE JOURNAL

I'm so happy and grateful for:

_____

_____

_____

I'm so happy & grateful *now* that:

_____

_____

_____

_____

_____

_____

_____

_____

_____

_____

_____

_____

_____

_____

_____

We're limitless unless we put boundaries on ourselves.

JOURNEY WELL, YOU ARE <u>MORE</u> THAN ENOUGH
GRATITUDE JOURNAL

I AM in alignment with my goals

I'm so happy and grateful for:

_____

_____

_____

I'm so happy & grateful *now* that:

_____

_____

_____

_____

_____

_____

_____

_____

_____

_____

_____

_____

_____

_____

_____

_____

JOURNEY WELL, YOU ARE <u>MORE</u> THAN ENOUGH
GRATITUDE JOURNAL

I'm so happy and grateful for:

_____

_____

_____

I'm so happy & grateful *now* that:

_____

_____

_____

_____

_____

_____

_____

_____

_____

_____

_____

_____

_____

_____

_____

_____

_____

The best way to defeat imposter syndrome is to listen to your inner cheerleader

instead and be grateful for your learned ability to recognize it.

JOURNEY WELL, YOU ARE <u>MORE</u> THAN ENOUGH
GRATITUDE JOURNAL

I AM a creator

I'm so happy and grateful for:

_____

_____

_____

I'm so happy & grateful *now* that:

_____

_____

_____

_____

_____

_____

_____

_____

_____

_____

_____

_____

_____

_____

_____

_____

_____

JOURNEY WELL, YOU ARE <u>MORE</u> THAN ENOUGH
GRATITUDE JOURNAL

I'm so happy and grateful for:

_____

_____

_____

I'm so happy & grateful *now* that:

_____

_____

_____

_____

_____

_____

_____

_____

_____

_____

_____

_____

_____

_____

_____

_____

The best way to create the better, brighter life you deserve is to love yourself.

I AM fun

I'm so happy and grateful for:

_____

_____

_____

I'm so happy & grateful *now* that:

_____

_____

_____

_____

_____

_____

_____

_____

_____

_____

_____

_____

_____

_____

_____

_____

_____

_____

JOURNEY WELL, YOU ARE <u>MORE</u> THAN ENOUGH
GRATITUDE JOURNAL

I'm so happy and grateful for:

_____

_____

_____

I'm so happy & grateful *now* that:

_____

_____

_____

_____

_____

_____

_____

_____

_____

_____

_____

_____

_____

_____

_____

_____

Imagine a world where there are NO mistakes, only lessons.

It's not only possible, it's waiting for you.

JOURNEY WELL, YOU ARE <u>MORE</u> THAN ENOUGH
GRATITUDE JOURNAL

I AM brave

I'm so happy and grateful for:

_____
_____
_____

I'm so happy & grateful *now* that:

_____
_____
_____
_____
_____
_____
_____
_____
_____
_____
_____
_____
_____
_____
_____
_____
_____

I'm so happy and grateful for:

_____

_____

_____

I'm so happy & grateful *now* that:

_____

_____

_____

_____

_____

_____

_____

_____

_____

_____

_____

_____

_____

_____

_____

_____

_____

_____

Gratitude as a way of life, when we give it to others,

returns to us in the meaningful and unexpected ways.

I AM calm

I'm so happy and grateful for:

_____

_____

_____

I'm so happy & grateful *now* that:

_____

_____

_____

_____

_____

_____

_____

_____

_____

_____

_____

_____

_____

_____

_____

_____

JOURNEY WELL, YOU ARE <u>MORE</u> THAN ENOUGH
GRATITUDE JOURNAL

I'm so happy and grateful for:

_____

_____

_____

I'm so happy & grateful *now* that:

_____

_____

_____

_____

_____

_____

_____

_____

_____

_____

_____

_____

_____

_____

_____

_____

_____

The truth you are afraid to say is the truth you must say.

I AM empowered

I'm so happy and grateful for:

_____

_____

_____

I'm so happy & grateful *now* that:

_____

_____

_____

_____

_____

_____

_____

_____

_____

_____

_____

_____

_____

_____

_____

_____

I'm so happy and grateful for:

_____

_____

_____

I'm so happy & grateful *now* that:

_____

_____

_____

_____

_____

_____

_____

_____

_____

_____

_____

_____

_____

_____

_____

_____

Giving = Living.

I AM amazing

I'm so happy and grateful for:

_____

_____

_____

I'm so happy & grateful *now* that:

_____

_____

_____

_____

_____

_____

_____

_____

_____

_____

_____

_____

_____

_____

_____

_____

_____

I'm so happy and grateful for:

_____

_____

_____

I'm so happy & grateful *now* that:

_____

_____

_____

_____

_____

_____

_____

_____

_____

_____

_____

_____

_____

_____

_____

_____

_____

_____

Serving others is the best way to secure the riches of your own contentment.

I AM compassionate

I'm so happy and grateful for:

_____
_____
_____

I'm so happy & grateful *now* that:

_____
_____
_____
_____
_____
_____
_____
_____
_____
_____
_____
_____
_____
_____
_____
_____
_____
_____

I'm so happy and grateful for:

_____

_____

_____

I'm so happy & grateful *now* that:

_____

_____

_____

_____

_____

_____

_____

_____

_____

_____

_____

_____

_____

_____

_____

_____

_____

_____

There's a grandeur, and joy, and affirmation, and beauty in every flight.

It's up to us to find it.

I AM fierce

I'm so happy and grateful for:

_____

_____

_____

I'm so happy & grateful *now* that:

_____

_____

_____

_____

_____

_____

_____

_____

_____

_____

_____

_____

_____

_____

_____

_____

_____

_____

JOURNEY WELL, YOU ARE <u>MORE</u> THAN ENOUGH
GRATITUDE JOURNAL

I'm so happy and grateful for:

_____

_____

_____

I'm so happy & grateful *now* that:

_____

_____

_____

_____

_____

_____

_____

_____

_____

_____

_____

_____

_____

_____

_____

_____

_____

Deep within us lies our True North. Become acquainted with the compass of your life.

JOURNEY WELL, YOU ARE <u>MORE</u> THAN ENOUGH
GRATITUDE JOURNAL

I AM open to receiving my gifts

I'm so happy and grateful for:

_____
_____
_____
_____

I'm so happy & grateful *now* that:

_____
_____
_____
_____
_____
_____
_____
_____
_____
_____
_____
_____
_____
_____
_____
_____
_____
_____

I'm so happy and grateful for:

_____

_____

_____

I'm so happy & grateful *now* that:

_____

_____

_____

_____

_____

_____

_____

_____

_____

_____

_____

_____

_____

_____

_____

_____

_____

_____

_____

Nothing is more difficult to erase than words we should have said.

I AM kind

I'm so happy and grateful for:

_____
_____
_____

I'm so happy & grateful *now* that:

_____
_____
_____
_____
_____
_____
_____
_____
_____
_____
_____
_____
_____
_____
_____
_____
_____
_____

I'm so happy and grateful for:

_____

_____

_____

I'm so happy & grateful *now* that:

_____

_____

_____

_____

_____

_____

_____

_____

_____

_____

_____

_____

_____

_____

_____

_____

_____

The most exciting and energizing part is that by sharing your gift,

you're helping to usher this new world into reality.

I AM curious

I'm so happy and grateful for:

_____
_____
_____

I'm so happy & grateful *now* that:

_____
_____
_____
_____
_____
_____
_____
_____
_____
_____
_____
_____
_____
_____
_____
_____

I'm so happy and grateful for:

_____

_____

_____

I'm so happy & grateful *now* that:

_____

_____

_____

_____

_____

_____

_____

_____

_____

_____

_____

_____

_____

_____

_____

_____

_____

As you live your hectic life, remember throughout the day to say, I AM More Than Enough.

I AM positive

I'm so happy and grateful for:

_____

_____

_____

I'm so happy & grateful *now* that:

_____

_____

_____

_____

_____

_____

_____

_____

_____

_____

_____

_____

_____

_____

_____

_____

_____

_____

I'm so happy and grateful for:

_____

_____

_____

I'm so happy & grateful *now* that:

_____

_____

_____

_____

_____

_____

_____

_____

_____

_____

_____

_____

_____

_____

_____

_____

The first victory is simply showing up, the next victory is not giving up.

I AM adaptable

I'm so happy and grateful for:

_____
_____
_____

I'm so happy & grateful *now* that:

_____
_____
_____
_____
_____
_____
_____
_____
_____
_____
_____
_____
_____
_____
_____
_____
_____

JOURNEY WELL, YOU ARE <u>MORE</u> THAN ENOUGH
GRATITUDE JOURNAL

I'm so happy and grateful for:

_____

_____

_____

I'm so happy & grateful *now* that:

_____

_____

_____

_____

_____

_____

_____

_____

_____

_____

_____

_____

_____

_____

_____

_____

_____

_____

Living with joy, gratitude, and appreciation in your life

will bring a contentment and ease to each day.

I **AM** different, and that's perfect

I'm so happy and grateful for:

_____
_____
_____

I'm so happy & grateful *now* that:

_____
_____
_____
_____
_____
_____
_____
_____
_____
_____
_____
_____
_____
_____
_____
_____

I'm so happy and grateful for:

_____

_____

_____

I'm so happy & grateful *now* that:

_____

_____

_____

_____

_____

_____

_____

_____

_____

_____

_____

_____

_____

_____

_____

_____

_____

_____

Choose to create an extraordinary life. You have what it takes. You are <u>More</u> Than Enough.

I AM courageous

I'm so happy and grateful for:

_____

_____

_____

I'm so happy & grateful *now* that:

_____

_____

_____

_____

_____

_____

_____

_____

_____

_____

_____

_____

_____

_____

_____

_____

I'm so happy and grateful for:

_____
_____
_____

I'm so happy & grateful *now* that:

_____
_____
_____
_____
_____
_____
_____
_____
_____
_____
_____
_____
_____
_____
_____
_____
_____
_____

Awaken and realize the way out is within.

I AM thoughtful

I'm so happy and grateful for:

_____

_____

_____

I'm so happy & grateful *now* that:

_____

_____

_____

_____

_____

_____

_____

_____

_____

_____

_____

_____

_____

_____

_____

I'm so happy and grateful for:

_____

_____

_____

I'm so happy & grateful *now* that:

_____

_____

_____

_____

_____

_____

_____

_____

_____

_____

_____

_____

_____

_____

_____

_____

_____

Gratitude journaling is something you've got to practice daily. Like taking a shower,

it only works if it's done regularly. It changes your life for the better.

I AM beautiful

I'm so happy and grateful for:

_____

_____

_____

I'm so happy & grateful *now* that:

_____

_____

_____

_____

_____

_____

_____

_____

_____

_____

_____

_____

_____

_____

_____

_____

JOURNEY WELL, YOU ARE <u>MORE</u> THAN ENOUGH
GRATITUDE JOURNAL

I'm so happy and grateful for:

_____

_____

_____

I'm so happy & grateful *now* that:

_____

_____

_____

_____

_____

_____

_____

_____

_____

_____

_____

_____

_____

_____

_____

_____

_____

_____

Your one wild and precious life must include taking what you learned,

and what you know, and giving it away.

I AM resourceful

I'm so happy and grateful for:

_____

_____

_____

_____

I'm so happy & grateful *now* that:

_____

_____

_____

_____

_____

_____

_____

_____

_____

_____

_____

_____

_____

_____

_____

_____

_____

_____

_____

I'm so happy and grateful for:

_____

_____

_____

I'm so happy & grateful *now* that:

_____

_____

_____

_____

_____

_____

_____

_____

_____

_____

_____

_____

_____

_____

_____

_____

_____

_____

Focusing on your desired goal, keeping your why in the forefront of your

thoughts and actions will automatically reveal the how.

I AM considerate

I'm so happy and grateful for:

_____

_____

_____

I'm so happy & grateful *now* that:

_____

_____

_____

_____

_____

_____

_____

_____

_____

_____

_____

_____

_____

_____

_____

_____

_____

I'm so happy and grateful for:

_____

_____

_____

I'm so happy & grateful *now* that:

_____

_____

_____

_____

_____

_____

_____

_____

_____

_____

_____

_____

_____

_____

_____

_____

_____

_____

Visioneering is just a fancy word for what some refer to as thinking from the end,

the method we suggest for you to create the better and brighter life for yourself.

I AM resilient

I'm so happy and grateful for:

_____
_____
_____

I'm so happy & grateful *now* that:

_____
_____
_____
_____
_____
_____
_____
_____
_____
_____
_____
_____
_____
_____
_____
_____
_____
_____
_____

I'm so happy and grateful for:

_____

_____

_____

I'm so happy & grateful *now* that:

_____

_____

_____

_____

_____

_____

_____

_____

_____

_____

_____

_____

_____

_____

_____

_____

_____

_____

We envision *Journey Well, You Are More Than Enough: (RE)Discover Your Passion, Purpose, & Love of Yourself & Life* as your flag of fire, your assumption of success giving you a powerful, uplifting message of hope.

I AM optimistic

I'm so happy and grateful for:

_____

_____

_____

I'm so happy & grateful *now* that:

_____

_____

_____

_____

_____

_____

_____

_____

_____

_____

_____

_____

_____

_____

_____

_____

_____

I'm so happy and grateful for:

_____

_____

_____

I'm so happy & grateful *now* that:

_____

_____

_____

_____

_____

_____

_____

_____

_____

_____

_____

_____

_____

_____

_____

_____

_____

_____

Success is an attitude, what you accomplish depends on you.

I AM fierce

I'm so happy and grateful for:

_____

_____

_____

_____

I'm so happy & grateful *now* that:

_____

_____

_____

_____

_____

_____

_____

_____

_____

_____

_____

_____

_____

_____

_____

_____

_____

_____

I'm so happy and grateful for:

_____

_____

_____

I'm so happy & grateful *now* that:

_____

_____

_____

_____

_____

_____

_____

_____

_____

_____

_____

_____

_____

_____

_____

_____

You're a highly creative person. The one and only you!

Give yourself an extra dose of gratitude today.

I AM confident

I'm so happy and grateful for:

_____
_____
_____
_____

I'm so happy & grateful *now* that:

_____
_____
_____
_____
_____
_____
_____
_____
_____
_____
_____
_____
_____
_____
_____
_____
_____
_____
_____

I'm so happy and grateful for:

_____

_____

_____

I'm so happy & grateful *now* that:

_____

_____

_____

_____

_____

_____

_____

_____

_____

_____

_____

_____

_____

_____

_____

_____

_____

Does your inner dialogue reflect your core values?

The echo in the canyon of your mind needs congruence and kindness.

I AM abundant

I'm so happy and grateful for:

_____
_____
_____

I'm so happy & grateful *now* that:

_____
_____
_____
_____
_____
_____
_____
_____
_____
_____
_____
_____
_____
_____
_____
_____
_____
_____

I'm so happy and grateful for:

_____

_____

_____

I'm so happy & grateful *now* that:

_____

_____

_____

_____

_____

_____

_____

_____

_____

_____

_____

_____

_____

_____

_____

_____

_____

_____

Everyone is fighting a battle we know nothing about. Always Choose Kind. ACK.

I AM focused

I'm so happy and grateful for:

_____

_____

_____

I'm so happy & grateful *now* that:

_____

_____

_____

_____

_____

_____

_____

_____

_____

_____

_____

_____

_____

_____

_____

_____

I'm so happy and grateful for:

_____

_____

_____

I'm so happy & grateful *now* that:

_____

_____

_____

_____

_____

_____

_____

_____

_____

_____

_____

_____

_____

_____

_____

_____

_____

You're not on this earth just to survive; you're here to thrive, to serve, to create, and to be happy.

I AM Strong & Worthy

I'm so happy and grateful for:

_____
_____
_____

I'm so happy & grateful *now* that:

_____
_____
_____
_____
_____
_____
_____
_____
_____
_____
_____
_____
_____
_____
_____
_____
_____
_____

I'm so happy and grateful for:

_____
_____
_____

I'm so happy & grateful *now* that:

_____
_____
_____
_____
_____
_____
_____
_____
_____
_____
_____
_____
_____
_____
_____
_____
_____

Being grateful tells the universe we're aware of the gifts we've been given,

and that we're prepared to give back in equal measure, or more!

I AM organized

I'm so happy and grateful for:

_____
_____
_____
_____

I'm so happy & grateful *now* that:

_____
_____
_____
_____
_____
_____
_____
_____
_____
_____
_____
_____
_____
_____
_____
_____
_____
_____

JOURNEY WELL, YOU ARE <u>MORE</u> THAN ENOUGH
GRATITUDE JOURNAL

I'm so happy and grateful for:

_____

_____

_____

I'm so happy & grateful *now* that:

_____

_____

_____

_____

_____

_____

_____

_____

_____

_____

_____

_____

_____

_____

_____

_____

_____

As you live your hectic life, remember throughout the day to say, I **AM** <u>More</u> Than Enough.

I AM fabulous

I'm so happy and grateful for:

_____
_____
_____

I'm so happy & grateful *now* that:

_____
_____
_____
_____
_____
_____
_____
_____
_____
_____
_____
_____
_____
_____
_____
_____

I'm so happy and grateful for:

_____

_____

_____

I'm so happy & grateful *now* that:

_____

_____

_____

_____

_____

_____

_____

_____

_____

_____

_____

_____

_____

_____

_____

_____

_____

The journey of life can change us in ways we never anticipated.

We have the ability to raise ourselves up with each decision we make.

I AM determined

I'm so happy and grateful for:

_____

_____

_____

I'm so happy & grateful *now* that:

_____

_____

_____

_____

_____

_____

_____

_____

_____

_____

_____

_____

_____

_____

_____

_____

_____

JOURNEY WELL, YOU ARE MORE THAN ENOUGH
GRATITUDE JOURNAL

I'm so happy and grateful for:

_____

_____

_____

I'm so happy & grateful *now* that:

_____

_____

_____

_____

_____

_____

_____

_____

_____

_____

_____

_____

_____

_____

_____

_____

_____

Each day we get to make a new choice on how we present to the world. Choose Wisely.

Be the amazing person you know you can be!

I AM appreciative

I'm so happy and grateful for:

_____

_____

_____

I'm so happy & grateful *now* that:

_____

_____

_____

_____

_____

_____

_____

_____

_____

_____

_____

_____

_____

_____

_____

_____

_____

_____

JOURNEY WELL, YOU ARE <u>MORE</u> THAN ENOUGH
GRATITUDE JOURNAL

I'm so happy and grateful for:

_____

_____

_____

I'm so happy & grateful *now* that:

_____

_____

_____

_____

_____

_____

_____

_____

_____

_____

_____

_____

_____

_____

_____

_____

This voyage of self-discovery is to be the most perilous and difficult trip you've taken.

And the most gratifying ever!

I AM energetic

I'm so happy and grateful for:

_____

_____

_____

I'm so happy & grateful *now* that:

_____

_____

_____

_____

_____

_____

_____

_____

_____

_____

_____

_____

_____

_____

_____

_____

I'm so happy and grateful for:

_____

_____

_____

I'm so happy & grateful *now* that:

_____

_____

_____

_____

_____

_____

_____

_____

_____

_____

_____

_____

_____

_____

_____

_____

_____

You get to choose the voice you listen to inside your head.

Make the message positive, affirming, and respectful.

JOURNEY WELL, YOU ARE <u>MORE</u> THAN ENOUGH
GRATITUDE JOURNAL

I AM present

I'm so happy and grateful for:

_____
_____
_____

I'm so happy & grateful *now* that:

_____
_____
_____
_____
_____
_____
_____
_____
_____
_____
_____
_____
_____
_____
_____
_____
_____
_____

I'm so happy and grateful for:

_____

_____

_____

I'm so happy & grateful *now* that:

_____

_____

_____

_____

_____

_____

_____

_____

_____

_____

_____

_____

_____

_____

_____

_____

_____

ACK, Always Choose Kind, a signal we use as an opportunity for kindness.

Remember kindness is a choice – especially to YOU!

I AM trustworthy

I'm so happy and grateful for:

_____

_____

_____

I'm so happy & grateful *now* that:

_____

_____

_____

_____

_____

_____

_____

_____

_____

_____

_____

_____

_____

_____

_____

_____

_____

_____

I'm so happy and grateful for:

_____

_____

_____

I'm so happy & grateful *now* that:

_____

_____

_____

_____

_____

_____

_____

_____

_____

_____

_____

_____

_____

_____

_____

_____

_____

Make sure the words you use with yourself are positive, supporting, and elevating.

Always choosing words that build yourself and others up is a key to creating a successful life.

I AM grateful

I'm so happy and grateful for:

_____
_____
_____

I'm so happy & grateful *now* that:

_____
_____
_____
_____
_____
_____
_____
_____
_____
_____
_____
_____
_____
_____
_____
_____
_____
_____

I'm so happy and grateful for:

_____

_____

_____

I'm so happy & grateful *now* that:

_____

_____

_____

_____

_____

_____

_____

_____

_____

_____

_____

_____

_____

_____

_____

_____

_____

Let energy flow to you and through you as you build a stronger, better, brighter world to live in.

JOURNEY WELL, YOU ARE <u>MORE</u> THAN ENOUGH
GRATITUDE JOURNAL

I AM inspired

I'm so happy and grateful for:

_____

_____

_____

I'm so happy & grateful *now* that:

_____

_____

_____

_____

_____

_____

_____

_____

_____

_____

_____

_____

_____

_____

_____

_____

_____

_____

JOURNEY WELL, YOU ARE <u>MORE</u> THAN ENOUGH
GRATITUDE JOURNAL

I'm so happy and grateful for:

_____

_____

_____

I'm so happy & grateful *now* that:

_____

_____

_____

_____

_____

_____

_____

_____

_____

_____

_____

_____

_____

_____

_____

_____

_____

The noise of the outside world is LOUD.

Take a few minutes each day to bring silence to yourself.

I AM skillful

I'm so happy and grateful for:

_____

_____

_____

_____

I'm so happy & grateful *now* that:

_____

_____

_____

_____

_____

_____

_____

_____

_____

_____

_____

_____

_____

_____

_____

_____

_____

_____

_____

JOURNEY WELL, YOU ARE <u>MORE</u> THAN ENOUGH
GRATITUDE JOURNAL

I'm so happy and grateful for:

_____

_____

_____

I'm so happy & grateful *now* that:

_____

_____

_____

_____

_____

_____

_____

_____

_____

_____

_____

_____

_____

_____

_____

_____

Treat yourself and others with dignity and respect, gratitude, and kindness.

You are a vital human being. You have great value. It's time for you to claim it.

I AM intelligent

I'm so happy and grateful for:

_____

_____

_____

I'm so happy & grateful *now* that:

_____

_____

_____

_____

_____

_____

_____

_____

_____

_____

_____

_____

_____

_____

_____

_____

_____

_____

I'm so happy and grateful for:

_____

_____

_____

I'm so happy & grateful *now* that:

_____

_____

_____

_____

_____

_____

_____

_____

_____

_____

_____

_____

_____

_____

_____

_____

_____

_____

Self-care practices work wonders at centering you, giving you serenity, and silencing the inner critic.

I AM dynamic

I'm so happy and grateful for:

_____
_____
_____

I'm so happy & grateful *now* that:

_____
_____
_____
_____
_____
_____
_____
_____
_____
_____
_____
_____
_____
_____
_____
_____
_____

I'm so happy and grateful for:

_____

_____

_____

I'm so happy & grateful *now* that:

_____

_____

_____

_____

_____

_____

_____

_____

_____

_____

_____

_____

_____

_____

_____

_____

_____

Our lives are our CV—our Complete Value. What we bring into the world, who we serve

with kindness, compassion, gratitude and respect, the values we share with others,

these are the parts of life that matter most, and make up our personal CV.

JOURNEY WELL, YOU ARE <u>MORE</u> THAN ENOUGH
GRATITUDE JOURNAL

I AM vibrant

I'm so happy and grateful for:

_____

_____

_____

I'm so happy & grateful *now* that:

_____

_____

_____

_____

_____

_____

_____

_____

_____

_____

_____

_____

_____

_____

_____

_____

_____

_____

I'm so happy and grateful for:

_____

_____

_____

I'm so happy & grateful *now* that:

_____

_____

_____

_____

_____

_____

_____

_____

_____

_____

_____

_____

_____

_____

_____

_____

_____

Your life is your gift. To you and those around you. Serve others in whatever capacity you can.

Giving = Receiving

I AM adventurous

I'm so happy and grateful for:

_____

_____

_____

I'm so happy & grateful *now* that:

_____

_____

_____

_____

_____

_____

_____

_____

_____

_____

_____

_____

_____

_____

_____

_____

_____

_____

I'm so happy and grateful for:

_____

_____

_____

I'm so happy & grateful *now* that:

_____

_____

_____

_____

_____

_____

_____

_____

_____

_____

_____

_____

_____

_____

_____

_____

Whatever follows I AM follows you.

Make sure it is worthy of you.

JOURNEY WELL, YOU ARE <u>MORE</u> THAN ENOUGH
GRATITUDE JOURNAL

I AM joyful

I'm so happy and grateful for:

_____

_____

_____

I'm so happy & grateful *now* that:

_____

_____

_____

_____

_____

_____

_____

_____

_____

_____

_____

_____

_____

_____

_____

_____

_____

I'm so happy and grateful for:

_____

_____

_____

I'm so happy & grateful *now* that:

_____

_____

_____

_____

_____

_____

_____

_____

_____

_____

_____

_____

_____

_____

_____

_____

_____

Raise your awareness. Words are important. Choose only positive ones to tell yourself.

Find the best in life.

JOURNEY WELL, YOU ARE <u>MORE</u> THAN ENOUGH
GRATITUDE JOURNAL

I AM <u>*MORE*</u> Than Enough!

I'm so happy and grateful for:

_____
_____
_____

I'm so happy & grateful *now* that:

_____
_____
_____
_____
_____
_____
_____
_____
_____
_____
_____
_____
_____
_____
_____
_____
_____
_____

JOURNEY WELL, YOU ARE <u>MORE</u> THAN ENOUGH
GRATITUDE JOURNAL

We're grateful you've trusted us to be your guide on this incredible journey of creating a better, brighter life for yourself and those around you. We're confident you're well on your way to finding what you've known is out there waiting for you.

Now that you've filled this journal, we highly recommend you continue building on the solid foundation you've laid for yourself. As we mentioned previously, we have a long-standing tradition of gratitude journaling twice daily. As you see from our energy and enthusiasm for life and the abundance we've created in our lives, gratitude journaling clearly works.

Fellow Traveler, we're grateful for you and wish you to

JOURNEY WELL

You Are <u>More</u> Than Enough,

Mariah & Byron Edgington

www.ingramcontent.com/pod-product-compliance
Lightning Source LLC
Chambersburg PA
CBHW052117020426
42335CB00021B/2796